CW01500584

BACK INTO DELIGHT

GRIEF RECOVERY AT THE SPEED OF LIFE

PAUL O'NEILL

To my family,

who have suffered beside me, and with whom I have suffered in return. For the laughter we've lost, and the love that remains.

To my friends,

who carry their own quiet heartbreaks, and still showed up. Your presence has been a kind of light.

To those who have lost someone dear—

and still ache. This is for the days you rise without knowing how.

For the memories that sting before they soothe. For the breath that catches. And the love that endures.

May this book meet you not with answers, but with recognition.

And may it help you find, in your own time, a way back into delight.

CONTENTS

NOTE TO THE READER

This book does not begin at the beginning.

It begins in the middle—of silence, of breath held too long, of names that once meant life and now mean loss. It does not follow a straight line. Neither does grief.

You won't find five stages in these pages. No checklist. No promise of closure. What you will find is something quieter, and perhaps more useful: a way back into movement. Into sensation. Into the small, stubborn rhythms that remind your body it hasn't disappeared.

You are not expected to read this in order. If Chapter One feels like too much, start with the tools. If your mind needs logic before emotion, begin at the end. The book will wait.

Everything here is drawn from lived experience—mine, and those I've sat beside. It's written for people who have fallen hard and are not interested in being told to stay down. People whose bodies have frozen in place, who can't yet cry but suspect they might laugh again, one day, if the conditions are right.

You don't have to believe in anything to begin. Just breathe. Or sigh. Or mutter a little. That's enough.

And if nothing else lands, let this truth settle somewhere beneath the ribs:

Grief warps, yes—*but so does recovery.*

It bends you toward delight, if you let it. Slowly. With practice. And often against your better judgement.

Welcome. Not to a solution, but to a stretch.

We begin not by pushing forward but by loosening what holds us still.

Paul O'Neill.

November 2022

PREFACE

I have outlived and buried my grandfathers, my father, my brother—and now, my son. That sentence shouldn't exist. No one should have to write one like it. But here it is, dragging itself across the page like a funeral that forgot how to stop. And no, I didn't grieve in five tidy stages. There was no emotional flatpack manual with step-by-step instructions and a helpful Allen key. Each loss twisted differently. Each grief brought its own peculiar weather: heavy skies, freak storms, long dry seasons of silence.

Until recently, my brother's death was the most bitter. A sharp, splintered grief that lodged under the ribs and refused to budge. It warped the shape of things—of me—and overstayed its welcome like miserable weather. What followed was an apprenticeship in grief. Not the kind with certificates and speeches, but the quiet kind—the kind that leaves you whispering questions into the dark and hoping someone, somewhere, answers.

Eventually, I got an answer—not one grand epiphany, but a series of half-lit discoveries. They helped me. And later, they helped others. I found myself sitting across from parents and partners who looked like I once had: crumpled, confused, cruelly aged by sorrow. They weren't broken, but their lives had buckled in odd, silent places. And I found, through trial, kindness, and sheer bloody-minded persistence, ways to help them unbuckle.

Then came the call. The kind that kicks the door off its hinges and spits in your face. My son—my boy—was gone. Sudden. Grisly. Without rehearsal. Grief didn't knock. It ransacked my psyche.

But here's the catch: this time, I wasn't the same man. I knew what was happening. I didn't feel wiser, tougher, or enlightened —if anything, I felt flayed. But I recognised the shape of the fall. I knew I wasn't beyond repair. Bruised, yes. Buckled, absolutely. But not broken. This time, I wasn't free-falling into some nameless abyss. I had a rope. I had, in places, a ladder. And as I hit bottom, I knew something lifesaving: I would be able to rise again.

Don't confuse that for optimism. This wasn't a pep talk in the mirror—it was bone-deep certainty. A whisper that outlasts the screaming. I knew I could laugh again one day—not because I was denying the loss, but because I'd learned how the body reopens itself to joy. Eventually. If you know how to ask.

Because grief isn't just a matter of heart or mind. It's a full-body event. A system-wide lockdown. The muscles tighten. The breath shortens. The face forgets how to soften. You don't choose the pit. Your body builds it. It's a well-meaning trap— reflex disguised as protection; protest disguised as pause. And it won't dismantle itself just because your brain delivers a seminar on resilience.

What's needed is a new reflex. A way to teach the body to let go —gently, deliberately, without betrayal. That's what I'd spent years learning: how to coax a bent frame back into joy. How to hold space for sorrow while inviting delight to pull up a chair. And now, after losing my son, I had to use it all. Every tool. Every breath.

So, I returned to what I'd already begun to shape: a recovery process that moves at the speed of *life*—not death. It doesn't ask you to get over anything. It helps you get through. I've named it *Back Into Delight*. It's not a miracle. It's not a shortcut. But it is a way out of the pit.

It begins by convincing the body. That's the first step—before journaling, before therapy, before meaning-making. You start by loosening the shoulders. Slowing the breath. Resetting the gaze. I've taught this to parents who thought they'd never rise again. And I've watched them laugh. Seen the light return behind their eyes—not because they forgot their child, but because they remembered themselves.

The goal isn't closure. It's contact. Reconnection. The ability to touch life again without flinching. And that doesn't happen in stages—it happens in signals. In reflexes. In tiny, recoverable moments that stack into something that feels, one day, like relief. And then, eventually, like joy.

So this is my vow: I will share what I've learned with every grieving parent and partner I can reach. I'll pass the rope. Lower the ladder. Sit beside the pit and wait until they're ready to rise. And when they do, I want them to find not just delight at the end of the tunnel, but the ability to create it wherever they go.

Because one less parent or partner in pain is not a small thing.

One more sibling or friend laughing is not a miracle—but it's close.

Back Into Delight is for them. For us. For anyone who's ever loved so much they thought the loss might drown them. It doesn't have to. Not forever. Not if we learn how to rise.

ONE
THE WARPING
THE TOLLS OF THE BELL

You don't notice the twist until everything tilts.

LATE THURSDAY NIGHT IN KILBURN, London, the sort of night where chip fat clings to your coat and the buses run late out of spite. I'd just come off shift, stinking of fryer oil and a bad mood, when Connor, my landlord, intercepted me in the hallway. He was usually as breezy as a bar stool regular—but tonight, he looked like he'd heard a bell ring and realised too late it was for someone he knew.

'There's been a call. From Scotland. You need to ring your dad. He's at your Uncle Ian's.'

No need for guesses. Grief doesn't ring twice without intent. I'd had a similar call five months earlier when Uncle John died— forty-nine, no warning, no ceremony. This one felt like a sequel with worse lighting and an uglier script.

Connor gestured toward the kitchen, a place usually reserved for bad tea and tepid conversation. I picked up the receiver like it was rigged to explode. My dad's voice came through—low, broken, as if each word had to negotiate its way out.

'Mark's dead. Road accident'.

I put the phone down slowly, as if the dial tone might reverse the news if I held on long enough. The house fell silent—but not the good kind. This was the kind of silence that presses against your ribs and dares you to breathe.

Everyone else was already there—Rosyth, Scotland—gathered in shock, clustered in proximity. I was in a city that didn't know me, let alone care. The loneliness wasn't poetic. It was practical. There wasn't even a shoulder to decline. So, I walked.

Out through Kilburn's street-lit grit, up the Edgware Road, nowhere in mind until my feet chose for me: *Sacred Heart Church*. The red doors were large and locked, which felt about right. I knocked. Nothing. I knocked again, as if god was hiding behind a curtain pretending not to be home.

So, I knelt on the steps. Cold, wet, indifferent. Not quite holy ground, but close enough for a boy with nothing else to stand on. I wept. I prayed. I cursed. I repeated Mark's name like a chant, as if repetition might resurrect.

He was just a boy—my brother—hit by a car on a quiet rural road, his life snapped like a twig on a blind bend.

The next morning, I booked a train north. Every mile felt like a bribe to reality, as if late arrival might change the ending. But the facts had beaten me there.

At the police station in Dunfermline, I found rage like some people find religion—sudden, righteous, and entirely uninvited. The desk sergeant offered procedural platitudes. No arrest. No charges. Just 'an accident'. I pounded my fist on the desk. It startled us both.

And then came my father, of all people, delivering mercy when I had come for fire. As though loyalty *after the fact* was a substitute for consequence, he said:

> *'She stayed with him until your mum arrived.*
> *That counts for something.'*

I raged:

> *'No, it doesn't! If she'd driven to the conditions,*
> *he'd still be alive. So, fuck her!'*

That was the first the bell really tolled for me. The first profound warping. Not a clean break. Not a poetic lesson in impermanence. It was a twisting. A buckling of something foundational. My timeline bent at that moment—not into tragedy, but into something harder to name. A quiet, persistent distortion in how the world moved. From that point on, nothing quite aligned the same.

THE BELL TOLLS AGAIN

It was a Friday morning in early November 2020. Sunlight hadn't yet made up its mind. I was still in bed, floating in that pre-conscious fog where dreams and duties argue about who goes first. Gillian entered the room slowly, the way people do when they're about to hand over a bomb and apologise for the inconvenience.

Her face said everything. Pale. Drawn. Eyes swollen from crying—or from knowing something the rest of the world hadn't yet caught up to. If sorrow had a uniform, she was wearing it.

And I, ever the optimist, braced for news of my mother. She was in her late seventies, after all, and had the sort of Catholic stamina that suggested death might need to negotiate. I thought it was her time. I was wrong. It wasn't my mother. It was my son. Kieran. Twenty-five. The age where you're still allowed to screw up but not expected to die.

I didn't say anything. Didn't cry. Didn't even blink. My head sank back into the pillow like it was trying to hide. Not the dramatic fall of a man shattered—just a slow-motion collapse. Like someone had pressed pause on gravity. I stared at the ceiling and began to fall behind my eyes.

Something in me went quiet. Not emotionally—mechanically. The kind of silence you notice when the fridge stops humming and the room becomes too still to feel safe. My breathing thinned out like it was being rationed. Each inhale an effort. Each exhale, a relief. The pauses between grew longer, like the body was considering early retirement.

And then, in the stillness, he appeared. Not as a ghost—nothing that poetic. More like a memory refusing to be archived. His strong frame. His soft voice. That lopsided grin he'd flash when trying not to laugh at his own jokes. I saw the tilt of his head. The familiar shuffle of his feet. The slow, deliberate kindness that made him unmistakably Kieran.

And that's when it hit—not the headline, but the footnote. The part grief saves for its second act. I would never see my son alive again. Not at Christmas. Not by accident in a shopping centre. Not even on a grainy phone screen. *Alive* was gone.

The sobbing came like hiccups—unexpected, ridiculous, impossible to stop. The kind of crying that rattles your bones and leaves you apologising to nobody. It jolted me back just enough to start asking questions. Not the practical ones—those came later—but the primitive ones: *When? How? Why?*

Gillian was already on the phone, conducting the necessary diplomacy of grief. The calls began: family, police, coroners— the endless bureaucracy of heartbreak. That night, I spoke to the coroner's office in Yorkshire. They had details. They always do.

'It happened on Friday 1st October, at 19:29,' they told me.

The specificity felt harsh. As if giving me the timetable somehow made it sound more controlled. Kieran had stepped in front of a train travelling at seventy miles per hour. The impact had scattered his body along the tracks for two hundred yards. His remains were identified by a fingerprint match on his game console. There's no good way to receive that information. But there are worse ways. I managed to find one.

Six weeks. That's how long he'd been in the mortuary freezer— unknown, unclaimed, untouched by the world that raised him. Six weeks of frostbite and forensic silence while we were none the wiser. And that's when the intellectual caught up to the emotional. I wouldn't just never see him alive again. I wouldn't see his face at all.

No final glance. No mortician's magic to restore a boy to something recognisable. The face I kissed goodnight, the cheeks I cupped in my hands—that face was gone. You don't bonce back from that. You move on, get passed it, by learning to move around it.

The Parallel Lines of Loss

Two phone calls. Thirty-five years apart. Same stomach drop. Same unnatural hush. Different damage.

Mark's death cracked something open. Kieran's collapsed the whole damn scaffolding.

One was combustion—external, righteous, loud. A thump on a sergeant's desk. Rage against a reckless driver. The other was implosion. No desk. No fists. No rage. Just the quiet folding-in of a man watching his own breath forget what it's for.

Mark left a howling void. Kieran left a silence so total it echoed. The grief was no longer storm—it was vacuum. A *pressureless* place where nothing grew and nothing broke, because everything had already bent.

And yet, they ran parallel. Not in content—Mark didn't choose his death; and Kieran did. But in shape. In how the world rearranged itself afterwards. In how my posture changed. In how the air shifted when I said their names out loud.

It would be tidy to say that Mark's death prepared me. It didn't. What it did was stretch the canvas so that, when the second bolt of lightning struck, it didn't tear straight through. It scorched something already warped. Grief leaves a watermark. You only see it when the next sorrow spills across the page.

I don't compare the two losses. That would be like ranking house fires. But I know this: grief has a memory. And when it returns, it doesn't start from scratch. It picks up where it left off —with sharper tools, crueller timings, no need to knock. If Mark's death punched a hole in the hull, Kieran's drove the ship under.

And yet, here I am—still telling it. Still above the waterline, if only just.

And somehow, still choosing not to sink.

The Unforgiving Timeline

Here's what no one tells you about grief: it's a time thief. Not just of the past, which it rewrites in smudged ink, but of the future, which it steals while you're still making plans. I thought I had more time. That line loops like bad hold music. I thought we'd talk. I thought we'd fix it.

I thought whatever this was—this distance, this drift—was temporary. A bit of youthful turbulence, not a final trajectory. I thought I had a *later*. I had *later* scheduled. Slotted. It was in the diary. But grief doesn't respect your calendar. It shows up early, kicks in the door, and rearranges your furniture while you're still asleep.

There were things unsaid, of course. Not because we were careless, but because life's momentum fools you into thinking there'll be another window. A quieter moment. A better mood. The right words. Instead, you get silence. Permanent. Absolute. The kind that closes a book mid-sentence and bolts the cover shut.

I could list regrets like receipts—the last conversation, the missed signals, the warnings I didn't hear until they echoed. But even if I had a ledger, it wouldn't change a thing. The trouble with finality is that it doesn't negotiate.

Grief isn't just about the person who's gone. It's about the future that vanished with them. The birthdays you won't attend. The apologies you won't give. The second chances that will never arrive. It's not only loss. It's interruption. Abrupt. Indelicate. Unfinished. And it's that *unfinishedness*—that hanging chord, that sentence without a full stop—that haunts the longest.

What the Body Knows

The mind takes notes. The body keeps score. I didn't learn that from a book. I learned it from my lungs, my skin, my spine. They logged both deaths with the precision of trauma's favourite stenographer: tension.

Mark's death taught me to flinch at late-night phone calls. Kieran's taught me to forget how to breathe. And not in the poetic sense—literally. My body decided that oxygen was optional, and silence preferable. Stillness—complete, paralysing stillness—felt safer than motion.

It wasn't a decision. There was no strategic withdrawal. No

moment of conscious choice. Just reflex—like touching something hot and pretending you didn't.

My face went numb. My limbs took on the texture of wet wool. My chest became a locked room with the key on the outside. This wasn't 'feeling sad'. This was a full-bodied rehearsal for death, choreographed by a nervous system convinced that grief was a threat best handled by shutdown.

People think grief is about crying. Sometimes. But more often, it's about *immobilisation*. About the body yanking every lever labelled *Don't Feel That*. And here's the rub: you can't out-think your own reflexes. You can't reason your way back to breath. The system that shut you down isn't taking advice from your better judgement.

It took me years to understand this after Mark—and only seconds to recognise it with Kieran. My body built a prison not because it was cruel, but because it was trying to keep me alive. Badly. Awkwardly. But sincerely. And like all prisons, the lock wasn't just on the outside. It was inside me too.

Two Graves, One Path Forward

Grief doesn't let you graduate. There's no certificate. No cap and gown. No return to the person you were before. At best, you become fluent in its dialect. You get better at navigating the terrain without tripping on the same stones. Mark is buried in Scotland. Kieran was cremated in England. But I carry them both in the same place. Not sentimentally—this isn't some Hallmark resurrection—but structurally. They rewired me. One changed the voltage. The other stripped the insulation.

I don't grieve them the same way. Mark's absence is a long shadow I've learned to walk beside. Kieran's is a minefield—I never quite know which thought will detonate the day. But here's the thing: I've stopped trying to win grief. Stopped treating it like a beast to conquer or a tunnel to sprint through. I no longer look for the end. I look for movement. Any movement. Forward, sideways, crawling—so long as it's not stillness.

Because stillness is where the body begins to turn to stone. And I've had enough of statues. Enough of shrink-wrapped emotions and respectable silence. Enough of smiling politely through funerals while my insides riot. I've chosen another path. Not heroic. Not glamorous. Just human.

When I speak to grieving parents now—those still kneeling outside locked church doors, those lying frozen under the weight of a name they can no longer say out loud—I don't offer comfort. I offer direction. I tell them what I had to learn by surviving it twice: that grief warps, yes—but it can be *unwarped*. Steadily. Carefully. With the same hands that once clenched in pain.

This is not resurrection. This is repair. One act at a time. One breath at a time. One honest moment, dragged from the pit and into the light. I thought we'd fix it—Kieran and I. I thought we had time. We didn't. So now I fix what I can. I fix myself. I fix others. I fix the broken stories we tell about grief and what comes after. I carry my son, not as weight, but as rhythm. And I walk on.

TWO

THE PIT & THE PRISON
FALLEN & LOCKED INSIDE

Stillness isn't peace. It's the body's barricade.

THE PIT ISN'T A METAPHOR. It's not poetic shorthand or some handy image lifted from Greek tragedy. It's real. Not a place you fall into, but a reflex your body builds before you even know you've left the surface.

It begins with silence—not the peaceful kind, but the sterile, clinical kind. The kind you hear in operating theatres and failed rescue attempts. In my case, it started the moment I heard Kieran's name in the same sentence as 'he's gone'. A sentence that, like some twisted incantation, drained all the air from the room and replaced it with concrete.

You think you'll scream. You don't. You think you'll fall to your knees. Maybe later. First comes the stillness. Not serenity—paralysis. The body stops mid-breath, as if hoping the news will reverse itself if you just hold still long enough. Muscles don't tense—they disappear. Speech doesn't falter—it vanishes. You're frozen in place like a paused video, waiting for the signal to resume.

And then, a strange sense of betrayal. Not by the world. Not even by god. By your own body. As if it's downed tools, called in sick, and left you behind the wheel. Eyes blink, but slowly. Breaths come, but reluctantly. Your limbs obey gravity more than will. You're technically present—but no one's home.

I didn't choose that. None of us do. The pit isn't made by thoughts. It's constructed by systems—automatic, ancient, brutally efficient. It's how we survive impact: switch everything off and hope the damage doesn't spread. It's not weakness. It's triage. And the worst part is—it works. For a while.

That's what makes it so convincing. That stillness, that numbness—it buys time. Time not to feel everything at once. Time to prevent the full collapse. It doesn't make the unbearable bearable. But it makes it liveable. Just.

But here's the cost. While the pit shields you, it also severs you. You stop feeling—but you also stop reaching. You stop crying—but you also stop connecting. The body doesn't distinguish between *pain* and *people*. It blocks them both, just to be safe. And before you know it, you're not just in a pit. You're in a prison.

OUR MAMMALIAN HEART

It helps to remember we're mammals. Hairy, social, needy mammals. We weren't designed for grandeur—we were designed to huddle. We find safety in faces, comfort in rhythm, regulation in company. And that's not poetic. That's wiring. We come pre-installed with a nervous system that asks a single question, thousands of times a day:

Am I safe enough to connect?

When the answer's yes, we lean in. We smile. We reach, joke, comfort. When it's no, everything shifts—voice tightens, eyes scan, limbs prepare. And if the answer's definitely not, we don't fight. We freeze. That's not a melodrama. That's physiology.

It's been tested, of course—lab rats, monkeys, the usual unlucky participants. In one study, animals were isolated, then shocked through the floor of the cage. Alone, they didn't resist. They didn't run. They curled up and endured. Shutdown, because freezing was the only available mercy.

Then they re-ran the experiment, but with two or more animals. Same shocks. Different result. This time, the rats fought—each other. Not because they'd become violent, but because the drive to connect had nowhere to go. No connection, no cooperation. No safety, no solidarity.

In human terms: if I don't feel safe, I can't reach you. If *you* don't feel safe, you can't reach me. Multiply that across a family and you get everyone drowning—with no lifeboats.

That's why, when grief hits a household, the room doesn't feel held. It feels like vacuum. Cold. Empty. Everyone's waiting for someone else to be the rock. The regulator. The still point. But no one's in position. The system's tripped its alarms and slammed every door.

People say grief brings us closer. Sometimes it does—*afterwards*. But in the first wave? It does the opposite. It breaks the signal. It tells the body:

Not now. Not them. Not safe.

And the worst part? It's invisible. You don't realise it's happening. You just feel unreachable. Or worse—unworthy of being reached. It's not your fault. It's your settings. Your nervous system has left the building. And it hasn't left a forwarding address.

That's when the prison starts to feel permanent. You can see the people you love. You just can't get to them. You're waving through bulletproof glass. And they're waving back—just as trapped.

The Prison Reflex

Shutdown is clever. Not noble, not romantic—just evolutionarily efficient. When the threat is too much, too fast, too sharp, the system doesn't hold a meeting. It doesn't check your diary or ask for permission. It pulls the emergency brake and kills the lights.

You freeze. Not in a dramatic, stage-left, spotlight-on kind of way. Just... subtly. Imperceptibly. The blink gets slower. The voice drops half an octave. You stare—not because you're pondering life's mysteries, but because you've been quietly evicted from your own body.

It's not a malfunction. It's a feature. Your system's way of saying:

'This is too much. Let's pretend we're not here'

And to be fair, it works—briefly. You don't feel the pain as sharply. You don't collapse in public. You avoid the wet, heaving sobs that sound like someone being throttled by their own throat. The daze saves you from that—for now.

But there's a cost. The longer you stay in shutdown, the more the daze becomes default. Your body forgets how to start again. You become a ghost in your own skin—ambulatory, polite, unreachably numb.

Shutdown is a savings account. The body banks the grief it can't afford to feel in real time. But like all savings accounts, it accrues interest. And eventually, you'll have to pay.

The prison doesn't feel like a trap at first. It feels like relief. Stillness instead of chaos. Silence instead of sobbing. But over time, the walls close in. The air thins. The comfort curdles into constraint. The numbness goes from helpful to harmful.

People ask, *'How are you doing?'* and you answer like a competent AI: coherent, flat, vaguely friendly. They nod. You nod. No one notices you haven't inhabited your body in days. Shutdown doesn't mean collapse. It's worse. Collapse would at least be loud. Shutdown is quiet. It's survival dressed up as coping. And unless you catch it—*really* catch it—it calcifies.

That's the prison reflex. Designed for protection. Brilliant for short-term damage control. Absolute hell long-term. Because the lock isn't on the outside. The door's open. You just can't move.

I'M NOT **Fucking Humpty Dumpty**

At some point—not day one, not even week one, but eventually —I looked in the mirror and said it aloud.

'I'm not fucking Humpty Dumpty.'

Not a battle cry. Not even loud. Just a dry, mutinous line muttered into the bathroom fog, aimed at no one in particular— except maybe the nursery-rhyme-shaped expectations squatting in my subconscious.

Because here's what I'd had enough of: the idea that some falls are final. That some griefs split you beyond repair and leave you politely shattered. You're done now. Please remain in pieces. And try not to leak sadness all over the carpet.

Well—no. I had fallen. Hard. Twice. And I was not a scrambled egg. I still had joints. I still had lungs. And somewhere inside the fog, I had a thread of something resembling will. Humpty Dumpty didn't get back up. But that's his problem. He sat there waiting for cavalry. Waiting for kings and horses. What exactly was the horse supposed to do—offer emotional support? Fetch glue?

That's not how this works. No one rides in. There's no magical grief unit funded by the crown. The cavalry is you, deciding to get vertical. So, I stood. Not in triumph—don't cue the swelling score. I moved more like an arthritic pensioner dismounting a low couch. But I stood.

Because no matter how warped I'd become, I still had tensile strength. I wasn't made of porcelain. I was made of scar tissue, stubbornness, and about a dozen bad metaphors. And most importantly—I'd been here before. Not this pit. Not this pain. But something like it. And what that gave me wasn't confidence. It was orientation. I didn't know the way out. But I knew the way up.

STRETCHING TOYS & Bending Spoons

I had a *Stretch Armstrong* when I was eight. Possibly the most honest toy ever made. No batteries. No lights. No marketing gimmicks. Just a flesh-coloured action figure filled with gel and attitude. You could stretch his arms, knot his legs, twist his torso into shapes that would get a human banned from yoga. And when you let go, he returned—slowly, stubbornly—to form.

Peering from over the *Daily Record*, my dad said,

> *'He's ductile. Also malleable. And elastic.'*

My dad, being a mechanical fitter, couldn't help himself. While I was testing the poor thing's limits, he was delivering a crash course in material science.

> *'Ductile means it stretches. Malleable means you can reshape it. Elastic means it bounces back.'*

He sipped his tea.

> *'Toughness is how much stress it can absorb without falling to bits.'*

Useful education, as it turned out. Because around that time, Uri Geller was on telly, bending spoons with his mind—or, more plausibly, his fingers and a well-practised smirk. Stretch Armstrong you could torture all day. A spoon? Bend it once and it stayed bent. Metal fatigue, they called it. Try and pull a spoon back into shape and it either warps or snaps.

Which, from a grief-recovery standpoint, is a significant design flaw. Here's the point:

I didn't want to be a spoon.
I wanted to be a *Stretch Armstrong*.·

I wanted my system—bruised, yes, knotted, absolutely—to return. Not untouched, but unbroken. So, I did what every enterprising child eventually does: I chucked him in the freezer.

After fifteen minutes, his limbs were reluctant. After an hour, he wouldn't budge at all. Like trying to wrestle a frozen sausage. He hadn't lost his strength—he'd just lost his give. And in that state—hardened, brittle, inert—he was easier to snap. Which, as it turned out, was a better metaphor than anything Uri Geller ever bent.

Because that's what happens when we freeze. We don't become stronger. We become fragile. We become objects that resist change until we shatter. Not because we're weak, but because we've lost our flexibility. Because stress, unabsorbed, accumulates in silence—until the wrong moment breaks everything.

But—and here's the quiet miracle—when I let the toy warm up again, he recovered. The gel softened. The limbs stretched. The resilience returned. Not because he tried harder. But because the conditions changed.

That's what recovery actually looks like. Not heroic struggle, but gentle thaw. Not some cinematic transformation, but a slow re-entry into motion, sensation, breath. You don't yank yourself back to life. You warm. You breathe. You yield. And eventually, you find your shape again.

From Prison to Path

Recovery didn't announce itself. It didn't knock politely or hand over a checklist. It began with something smaller. Something embarrassingly ordinary. A breath. Not a deep one. Just a slightly less shallow one. The kind that doesn't feel like a negotiation. The kind that arrives uninvited and, mercifully, doesn't leave. One breath that didn't stick in my throat. That didn't feel like betrayal.

That's how it starts. Not with a plan, or a mantra, or an inspirational quote slapped on a mug. But with a flicker of life in a body that had gone quiet. The prison doesn't open with a clang. It eases. And when it does, what you need isn't a battle cry. You need warmth. Movement. Humour, if you can manage it. A sarcastic mutter. A stretch.

Grief froze me, yes. But I thawed. Slowly. Repeatedly. Sometimes against my will. I didn't march out of that pit. I sidled. I crawled. I fumbled toward sensation like someone reaching for the light switch in a power cut.

And I kept reminding myself—sometimes aloud, often with a smirk—*I'm not fucking Humpty Dumpty*. I don't need to be put back together. I need to move again. To soften. To flex. I need, in short, to become a little more like that toy from the seventies —gel-filled, odd-looking, indestructible on a good day.

Because recovery isn't about perfection. It's about range. The capacity to stretch without breaking. To return, not to who you were, but to motion. And the ability to stretch again—that's where walking out of the prison begins.

THREE

THE TOOLS & THE TOYS
PULLING YOU FORWARD

If the world won't send the signal—<u>you must</u>.

NOT ALL WARPING IS DAMAGE.

In sailing, to *warp* a vessel means to throw an anchor in the direction you want to go. Once it bites, you haul yourself forward—not by engine or sail, but by stubbornness. It's not glamorous. It's deliberate.

The kind of motion you earn.

That image stuck with me. Because after grief hits, you're not exactly adrift—you're grounded in the worst way. Flat. Motionless. Not broken, just stuck somewhere between breath and no breath, waiting for the atmosphere to change. But here's the snag: *it doesn't.*

Not unless you change it.

THE BODY CAN'T SHIFT UNTIL THE SIGNAL CHANGES

(Why recovery is about cues, not time)

"If that signal doesn't arrive from the outside, you'll have to learn how to send it from within."

YOU SEE, BIOLOGY DOESN'T COME WITH A WRISTWATCH. It doesn't care how long it's been since the trauma, the funeral, or the final conversation you'll never get to fix. If the environment still reads 'unsafe', the system stays locked. The drawbridge doesn't lower just because you've scheduled healing for Tuesday at 3 p.m.

That's the cruel precision of it. Even after the danger has passed, your body won't shift unless it receives an all-clear. And if that signal doesn't arrive from the outside, you'll have to learn how to send it from within.

No small ask. Especially when everything inside you has curled in on itself like a startled hedgehog and would very much prefer to stay that way.

But there's good news, even if it arrives dressed in overalls and smelling faintly of antiseptic and defiance. You don't need one perfect method. There isn't a single sacred practice known only to Himalayan monks and former SAS captains. What you need is a kit—a jumble of breath, laughter, tone, movement, stillness, and the ability to get a little absurd at the right moment.

Some of these are tools. Others are toys. All of them are cues—ways to tell your system, quietly and convincingly:

You're safe now. You can come back home.

This section is a rummage through that kit. A guided tour of the things that helped me—and the people I've walked with—shift from shutdown to stretch. They're not foolproof. But they are field-tested. And if used with even half a smile, they might just pull you forward.

Not heroically. Not in slow motion. But enough. Enough to rise. Enough to laugh again. Enough to breathe like someone who isn't bracing for impact. And that's how we begin to move again —not at light speed, perhaps. But at *life speed.*

BREATH: **The Quiet Commander**

(The nervous system's first responder)

> *"You can't breathe deeply and panic at the same time."*

Breath is the oldest medicine we have. Older than language, older than tools, older than the first story scrawled in charcoal on a cave wall. Long before we had names for grief or shame or rage, we had breath. And when everything else was taken— home, hope, son—it was the one thing left I could still do. Just.

The trick, of course, is remembering to use it before your nervous system decides to stage a walkout.

I learned the mechanics of breathing—not the obvious in-and-out, but the subterranean stuff—from Michael Grinder, a man who could read a room like it owed him rent. He taught me to notice where the breath sits. Not philosophically. Physically.

*Does it settle low, moving the belly in and out
    like a tide?*

*Or does it cling to the chest, shallow and twitchy,
    like a squirrel in a thunderstorm?*

It turns out, breath placement is not just a tell. It's *the* tell. A quietly precise gauge of where someone's body believes they are —even if their words are insisting everything's fine. A low belly breath says: safe, steady, connected. A high, fast chest breath says: get ready to bolt, something's about to eat us.

It's wonderfully democratic. You can't bluff it. Breath doesn't lie. Most people don't realise they're holding their breath until you catch them in the act—mid-sentence, mid-worry, mid-funeral. So when I work with someone in distress, we don't start with philosophy. We start with oxygen.

Sighs, Noodles, and Monarchs

(Using breath with mischief to soften the system)

> *"Seriousness is just anxiety in a tailored suit."*

Now, this is where it gets a little ridiculous—which is precisely the point. I'll look them dead in the eye and say:

> 'Let's do the King Henry VIII sigh'

They look at me, sceptically. I demonstrate. Sharp inhale. Full, dramatic exhale. A long 'Aahhhhh!!', with all the theatrical pomp of a monarch who's just had a second helping of roast swan and needs the peasants to notice. It's loud, lazy, and entirely unserious. Which makes it perfect.

> *Because seriousness is just anxiety in a tailored suit.*

They'll give me a feeble version in return. I'll look appalled.

> *'No, no. That won't do. I said Henry VIII, not Prince Edward. Lavish. Be regal about it.'*

We go again. Bigger, louder, sillier. And then, inevitably, something breaks—a chuckle, a crack in the armour, a momentary return of warmth to the cheeks. The body remembers it doesn't have to be in a trench. We follow that with the opposite: slow breath out, like a thread of smoke. No tension. No grit. Just time stretching itself out again.

Then comes the *noodle trick*—breathe in as if you're slurping a noodle from the bowl. It's stupid. It's effective. It guarantees a belly breath. And it usually comes with a smile, which is the real point. A body that can play is a body that isn't scared.

Because here's the quiet miracle: when you breathe deeply into your tummy, panic begins lessen and dissipates. Breath is the signal system beneath the signal system. You breathe low, and your body starts cancelling the alarms it had already called in. Sirens dim. Lights flicker off. It's over. You're here. You're safe enough to exhale.

We think of breath as background. It isn't. It's command. The first and last rhythm we ever learn. And if we can learn to listen for it—not just in crisis but in daily life—we gain something better than calm. We gain control.

Humour: **The Unauthorised Healer**

(*Disarming shame through laughter and permission*)

> *"Not a distraction. An infiltration."*

If breath is the quiet commander, humour is the saboteur behind enemy lines—slipping past the guards of self-seriousness, dismantling the explosives of shame, and loosening the bolts on whatever mental scaffolding has been holding up your pain. It's not a distraction. It's infiltration. But you have to earn your way in.

You can't lead with the punchline—not when someone's still holding their breath like it might be the last clean thing they own. The body doesn't trust quickly. Neither does the part of the mind that's been running loss simulations in the background since childhood.

So you start small. Face to face. Shared eye contact. Mutual rhythm. A sigh. A *noodle-breath*. Then—if the weather holds—you crack the door for mischief.

That's where I bring in Grinder's idea of *permission*. Not the legal kind. Not even the formal kind. The subtle kind that flickers in the corner of a mouth. Say something odd. If they smile, you're in. If they don't, you're not. Rapport gets you to the door. Permission gets you through it.

Like the gregarious young lawyer who came to me with an interesting phobia—odd enough to make a diagnostic manual reach for a dram. He felt fear when he met a woman to which he was attracted. I told him his phobia was so ironic that it had two names, presumably so sufferers could go for whichever one they found *least* attractive. He smiled. Rapport intact. So I carried on.

I told him about my puppy. A big black dog had startled it with an overly intimate greeting—cold nose, back end, no warning. Ever since, the puppy had taken to avoiding big black dogs with the urgency of a hungover commuter spotting a fare inspector. I added:

> *'Much like you: skilfully evading any woman*
> *you find attractive.'*

He smiled again. Slightly wider. I said:

> *'At least, my puppy avoids things he* doesn't
> *want!'*

Now we were properly orbiting his pattern. I said,

> *'You've been shying away from the thing you*
> *long for, as if it might jump out and kick you.*
>
> *This is pattern too human to be accidental and*
> *too silly to remain sacred.'*

His smile had turned into a grin. I said,

> *'Because only a human, would spend years*
> *searching for the thing they most desire... and*
> *then leg it as soon as it shows up, in order...'*

He finished the sentence for me:

> *'...to avoid it!'*

Then we both laughed. Not kindly. Not cruelly. Just clearly. With relief.

Laughter as Leverage

(From avoidance to pattern play)

> *"Only a human would search for the thing they most desire... and then leg it as soon as it shows up."*

I switched into a mock-German accent.

> *'So,' I asked, 'when you were young, did an attractive lady sneak up and startle you—like the black dog did to my puppy?'*

He laughed again, properly this time, and said no. I shrugged,

> *'Well then, maybe there's something else to it.'*

Permission maintained. Pattern exposed. Laughter engaged. From there, the conversation could deepen. We agreed—though mostly with our eyes—that this avoidance trick, while excellent for preserving nerves, was spectacularly useless for finding a soulmate.

I asked what came to mind when I'd first described the puppy. He said he'd visualised the exact scene—puppy startled, tail clamped, mid-walk horror. Then, with a spark of absurdity, imagined a woman with a cold wet nose. He giggled. Then laughed. Then paused. Because something had shifted.

Humour doesn't fix the pattern. Not on its own. But it destabilises it. It puts a dent in the authority of the reflex. The moment you can laugh at your pattern, you're no longer obeying it. The spell is broken. Not undone, not erased, but named. And named things, as we know, can be changed.

By now, they've usually started to breathe lower. Their posture is less military. The face has returned from furlough. And just beneath the laughter, something almost magical begins: *the reactivation of choice.*

Humour has done its job. Not as anaesthetic—but as invitation. The work that follows? That's where we turn *niggles into giggles.* And that's when change stops feeling like surgery and starts feeling like sabotage.

Voice: **The Volume Knob of Safety**

(*Prosody and the nervous system's hidden translator*)

> *"I take care. I speak in a very particular way."*

It's a curious thing—how easily mammals tune each other out. Not with malice. Not even with effort. Just through biology doing its ancient job. When danger edges into the room—real or remembered—the nervous system draws the curtains and changes the station. Normal conversation? Too middle. Too civilised. Too unhelpful. It vanishes into static.

Dr. Stephen Porges gave it a name: *neuroception.* But long before theory arrived with a lab coat and a graph, our ancestors already knew. When the body thinks it might be lunch, it tunes its ears for growls and alarms, not wedding toasts and bedtime stories.

High notes. Low notes. Anything in the middle—most of human speech, for instance—gets filtered like bad wine. Which makes things awkward when your job is to help people *hear* themselves.

Clients arrive mid-flood. Breath high. Shoulders like scaffolding. Language barely clinging to grammar. And though they're technically nodding, I can tell the words aren't landing. Not properly. Not down in the part of them that matters. The part that might actually help.

Now, I could raise my voice. Shout. Wave my arms like a caffeinated flight attendant. Or—I could do the opposite. I lower my tone. Slow my cadence. Drop the pitch by a fraction and stretch the vowels like warm taffy.

Not because it sounds nice (though it does), but because the middle range—the calm, melodic, prosodic range—is where the body learns to trust again. So I draw their attention to the sound itself. Not the content. The *carrier*.

I tell them:

'My voice doesn't just travel from my mouth to your ears. It wraps around you like a soft cone of healing sound. And because of that, I take care. I speak in a very particular way. Every sentence begins a little higher... and ends a little lower. Every word is part of a rhythm, every syllable tuned just so. And you'll find, as you listen, that this shape—this rise and fall—helps you settle, calm and begin to relax.'

EARNING **Attention with Rhythm**

(Melody as metronome, not manipulation)

> "Voice doesn't command attention. It earns it."

THEY USUALLY BLINK AT THAT. Not because they don't believe me—but because some part of them already knows. They've felt it before. A parent's lullaby. A teacher who could calm a room with a sentence. A friend who didn't panic when you did.

It's not magic. It's engineering. Acoustic scaffolding for a nervous system under siege. And so, while they follow my instructions—on the inside, thoroughly—my voice keeps doing its work on the outside. A metronome of safety. A tether to now. A permission slip for their body to put down its arms.

Only once they've heard me fully—not just with ears, but with skin and breath and posture—are they ready. Not for conversation. For trance. Because that's the real trick of voice control: it doesn't command attention. It earns it.

Trance: **The Gentle Technology of Change**

(*Teaching the body what safety feels like—again*)

> "*Reality, but better ventilated."*

The moment a client closes their eyes, something ancient stirs. Not theatre. Not mysticism. Just a quiet contract with their body: for the next few minutes, they don't have to monitor the exits, because they are safe here with me.

We begin at the scalp—not because it's the most stressed, but because no one ever thinks to start there. The client is asked to feel into it. Not just vaguely. Not just in passing. I want them to scan each muscle like they've been hired to audit it. I say:

'Even though you might think the muscles of the scalp are flat, they're still three-dimensional. Which means every single one has a top and bottom, a left and right, a front and back. Don't leave any side out.'

There's a pause as they begin. Then, one word:

'*Soften*'

They say it to themselves—not loudly, not theatrically. But ever so softly; ever so gently. Like they are soothing someone that they love deep inside, at the back of their mind.

It's somewhere between a command and a suggestion, it's a soothing invitation to their body to let go of what it is they don't need anymore.

And like all the gentle commands, it's not shouted, it's calm. And then followed, calmly and gently, by their softening body.

We work our way down—forehead, jaw, neck, shoulders— slowly, deliberately, like someone deactivating landmines they didn't know they were carrying. With each body part, I give a fact or two. Something real. Something anatomical. Something they know and sense, and feel.

Because trance, when done well, doesn't float you away—it tethers you more deeply to the *now*, which is the present. Reality, but better ventilated.

Somatic Precision

(*From scalp to breath, the body learns it's safe*)

"*You don't float away—you tether more deeply to the present.*"

And all the while, I speak in that same melodic voice: the one tuned for trust, the one we rehearsed together. Up at the start of the sentence, down at the end. A wave, not a hammer. A lullaby for the sympathetic nervous system. It doesn't take long.

Even first-timers—those who arrived doubtful, arms crossed metaphorically or literally—notice it. The slackening. The spread of stillness. That subtle surprise when they realise they've moved from thinking about their body to inhabiting it. Properly. Maybe for the first time in years.

When we return—because trance is always a return, never an escape—I ask them to clench their hands. Not tightly. Just enough. Enough to calibrate what relaxation now feels like, by comparing it to tension on demand. It's the somatic equivalent of bolding a word so the others seem clearer.

They're ready now. Not for insight. Not even for change. For *training*.

Because what comes next isn't vague affirmation or dreamy suggestion. It's rigorous. It's designed. It's the work I learned, directly, from Dr Richard Bandler—the co-founder of Neuro-Linguistic Programming—whose exercises make the extraordinary learnable, and the learnable unforgettable.

The client's body knows how to relax. Their breath knows where to go. Their voice, eventually, will return with new rhythm. But for now, they're open. They're listening. And more importantly—they're ready. Because trance doesn't impose change. It clears the space and primes the body for it.

THE FATE REVERSAL Toolkit

(Editing emotional memory through NHR)

> "Spin it backwards. Add clown music.
> Shrink the image. Flick it away."

Carl Jung once said,

> *'Until you make the unconscious conscious, it
> will direct your life and you will call it fate.'*

He had a flair for understatement. Most people spend decades being steered around by mental phantoms they haven't even formally met. Like getting punched repeatedly by an invisible man and blaming the breeze. So, we introduce them.

That's the real job here. Not insight. Not catharsis. Introduction. To show the client that the thing they dread—the flashback, the panic, the spider—isn't out there. It's in here. More precisely, in *there*—in the head, in the gut, in the body's cinema, looping its favourite horror reel on high volume with surround sound.

But here's the twist: once that reel is playing consciously, it can be redirected. That's where *Neuro-Hypnotic Repatterning* (NHR) comes in. Or, as I like to call it: emotional editing for grown-ups who've realised the first cut wasn't the final one.

We start with calibration. Not from me—but from them. Breath already slowed, posture softened, the client is invited to call up the troublesome image. Not describe it. Not unpack it. Just *relive* it. In colour, in sound, in sensation.

> 'See what you saw, hear what you heard, feel
>   what you felt.'

I move my chair to the side—not out of the way, but out of the frame. Because this is their theatre now, and I'm not here to direct. I'm here to coach the lighting crew. Their body will tell me everything I need to know. Facial tension. Lip colour. The sudden stillness that isn't peace, but anticipation. We're on.

I tell them plainly:

> 'I know this is unpleasant. I also know that,
>   before we're done, you'll learn how to take
>   command of what used to scare you. And
>   you'll get good at it. Possibly faster than is
>   polite.'

We intensify the feeling. Turn the volume up, not to punish them, but to make the wiring easier to find. Then I ask:

> 'All emotion is a motion. It has to move through
>   your boy. So, where in your body does it
>   begin?
>
> Where does it move to next - does it go up or
>   down, left or right, back or forward?
>
> Take your hand and show me'

They don't analyse. They *trace*. Their hand might start to map the route—gut to chest, chest to throat. The nervous system, made visible.

Then: colour it. What colour is the feeling? Yes, that one. No, don't think—just name it. And now, pull it out. Turn it around. Make it move in the opposite direction. Give it a new colour—one that suits recovery, not collapse—and bring it back in.

By this point, the old circuit is scrambled. Still active, yes—but no longer obeying its previous logic. Now I overlay the good feeling. Breathe low. Spin it up. Only when they can *sustain* this state—really hold it—do they open their eyes. And then we begin the mischief. I say:

> 'Go to the end of that memory, and now... play it
> backwards. At double speed. With clown
> music.'

There's often a blink. A scoff. Sometimes a bark of laughter. Excellent. That means the association is loosening its grip.

Pattern Sabotage, Not Catharsis

(When emotional rewiring meets ridiculous precision)

"The spell is broken. Not undone. Not erased. But named."

Then we drain the colour—black and white. Shrink it down to the size of a crumb. Flick it away like a dead pixel on a windscreen. We repeat - five times faster and faster. Recall. Recalibrate.

> 'Now think of the bad experience. What's
> different?'

Usually, everything. Because phobias, fears, grief and traumas-that-won't-quit—they all have one thing in common: they rely on being treated as through they are *permanent*. Immutable. Just the way things are and will always be.

This exercise, delivered with a wink and a scalpel, reveals a different truth. That fate can be coached. That fear can be retrained. And that sad and scary thoughts, properly mocked, properly re-spun, properly filed, can become controlled. With a different ending.

BECOMING a White-Belt at Bliss

(Why joy is a muscle you rehearse, not a mood you wait for)

> "You were a black-belt at bad feelings...
> now you're a white-belt at good ones."

BY THIS STAGE in the work, the client is no longer simply 'present'. They're tuned. Tilted slightly. Loosened at the edges. The old reflexes aren't gone—they're waiting in the wings—but what's changed is the lighting on the stage. Brighter in some places. Softer in others. The inner world has begun, finally, to listen to a different voice.

And now comes the part that looks like magic but isn't. Not really. But *you really feel that it is.*

With the client already in a gentle altered state—shoulders lower, breath smooth, facial tension gone walkabout—we slip seamlessly into deeper waters. No bells, no whistles. Just the continued flow of carefully chosen words, timed with the precision of a locksmith.

Because the right voice, at the right rhythm, helps you trip the lock from the inside. I heard, Richard Bandler, never one to waste a good rhyme, say once,

> 'It's the surface of your skin is where it really
> begins. So let that good feeling begin to
> spin.'

It sounds simple—nursery-rhyme simple—but don't be fooled. Simplicity is often a disguise worn by genius when it wants to be invited in. The cadence, the consonance, the rhyme: they're not flourishes. They're crowbars. And in the right hands, they pry open the body's oldest vaults.

Because once your body knows how to engage with it, you can spin the good feeling faster; and amplify... intensify... and multiply the good feeling more. And what was once a beautiful calming sensation in one part of your body, can begin to expand and be felt all over your body.

Because, just like grief, blissful calm isn't just a matter of heart or mind. It's a full-body event. A system-wide release. The muscles soften. The breath deepens. The tongue drops. The lips curl up into a little smile. And the clouds can be warmed away by delight.

ANCHORING CALM with Instruction

(*Embedding the state—not just visiting it*)

> "Bliss isn't random. It's trainable. Just like panic was."

Now, in this deeper lovelier altered state, we can anchor not just calm, but *calm with instructions*. We don't simply observe the bliss—we learn to steer it. The client is invited to discover how that warmth, that softness, that subtle hum of wellbeing travels through their body. And once they can trace it, they can amplify it. And once they can amplify it, they can *practice* it.

Because here's the kicker: bliss isn't random. It's trainable. Just like panic was. I'll say, matter-of-factly:

> 'You were a black-belt at bad feelings, because
> you practised. Relentlessly. Over and over,
> you rehearsed them until they showed up on
> command.'

Then comes the tilt. The pivot from lament to leverage.

> 'But now, you're a white-belt at good ones.
> You've just begun. And to get as good at joy
> as you were at dread, you'll have to practise.
> Lavishly. Repeatedly. Willingly. Not just out
> of discipline, but out of design.'

What we are building here isn't just comfort. It's a particular kind *durability*. A neuro-resilience where the client is no longer subject to the weather system of their nervous system. They're learning to forecast it. To warm it. To command it. To take control of it.

And so I ask—not sternly, not sentimentally, but with absolute clarity:

> 'I would like your unconscious to do this again
> and again. In all the rests of your life. Auto-

*nomically. Quietly. Confidently. So that you
remember to feel good many a times.
Whether it's a calm daze... or whether it's a
restful night.'*

Safety Isn't the Absence of Fear

(What deep resilience actually sounds like)

"Softly, steadily, with skill—even on the worst days"

There is no grand finale. No cymbal crash. Just a softened breath, a slight smile, and the sense—felt, not forced—that something once brittle has begun to loosen, to soften, to begin to bend easily and come back into the right shape again.

Because deep safety isn't about absence of fear. It's about knowing you can return to yourself—softly, steadily, with skill. Even on the worst days.

Especially on the worst days.

FOUR
THE DAWN
THE ELASTIC RETURN

You don't return by trying harder.
You return by *softening*.

THE BEND ISN'T NOTICED until you realise that the world has stops fitting. Grief doesn't announce that it's warped your internal scaffolding. It just carries on as though the angles were always like this—as though your chest was always this tight, your smile always this slow, your dreams always this dim.

You keep showing up, half a degree off true, wondering why nothing quite aligns. You're not broken. You're bent. And not metaphorically, either. Physically, neurologically, emotionally— warped by the force of impact. But here's the quiet miracle: *warped is not the same as ruined*.

Resilience, when it's real, isn't about standing tall while the winds howl. It's about the ability to return—not to some pristine, untroubled state, but to functional alignment. To come back into shape after the blow. To spring, not snap.

This, at its core, is what we mean by *elasticity*—the difference between being fragile and being alive. You don't build it through slogans. You build it by learning how to bring your system home. Again and again, without losing your keys or your courage. And the trick isn't brute strength. It's responsiveness.

Most people think resilience is about toughness. That's fine, if you're a steel beam or a Marvel character. But humans are not beams. We're more like tendon and memory foam. We *absorb*. We stretch. We give. And then, if we're trained, we return. But returning—*really* returning—requires more than time. It requires signal.

This is where most self-help hits a brick wall. It tells you to 'bounce back', but forgets to mention how. It offers affirmations, but skips the bit about your nervous system needing more than inspirational wallpaper.

You don't bounce back just because you want to. You bounce back when your biology agrees that it's safe to do so. And biology, being awkward, doesn't take orders. It takes cues.

This is the core skill resilient people have learned: how to generate their own internal cues of safety when the external ones have gone missing. It's not magic. It's method. A process of reactivating your own socialised bio-setup—what the body does when it believes the lion has finally left the building. What it does when it's time to live again.

This is what separates recovery from mere survival. The difference between being technically alive and genuinely open to life as it arrives. Resilient people can rupture and repair quickly. They can flex under pressure without deforming. They come back online before the damage calcifies. And, crucially, they can do so often enough that the warp never becomes permanent.

What this means in practice is deceptively simple: they've learned to listen for the shutdown *before* it seals the vault. They catch the shallow breath, the dry mouth, the narrowing eyes. And instead of waiting for collapse, they move. They *intervene*. Not by pushing through, but by pulling in the signal—by breathing low, softening the jaw, dropping the tongue, loosening the pelvic floor, and letting the body know: it's safe now. Not because someone else said so. Because they *made* it so.

This is how trauma gets resolved. Not overwritten. Not denied. But rendered unnecessary—because the rupture was caught, cushioned, and repaired before the break became brittle. The bend was met with give. And so it did not crack.

Resilience is not a posture. It's a *process*. A return to shape—sometimes slowly, sometimes defiantly, always deliberately. And once you've learned it, the shape of you stops being a victim of circumstance. It becomes a decision. A discipline. You stop waiting for the world to grant you peace. And you start bringing it with you.

THE FLUID SIGNALS

It begins in the mouth. Not with words, but with what's missing: saliva. A dryness so sudden it might as well be a sandstorm. Not thirst. Not dehydration. Just a silent, slightly sticky clue: your system no longer thinks it's safe to digest.

This is how the body speaks before language—through fluids, or their absence. Tears, saliva, mucus: the unloved stepchildren of biology. Socially discouraged, quietly ignored, functionally essential. You can tell someone's inner world by their outer moisture. Crying isn't just grief leaking out—it's cortisol draining. A wet mouth isn't just hydration—it's a physiological green light, a nod from your system saying,

'We're good. Carry on with the living.'

But when threat looms—real or remembered—your mucous membranes panic. Moisture retreats. The tongue lifts. The eyes dry. The nose tightens. And you are back in the war zone, even if the battle's long over.

This is what I call the fluid code. And the code doesn't lie.

The elementary system—the oldest part of our internal operations manual—tracks safety by flow. Safety *feels* like wetness. You can't fake it. You can't affirm your way into it. The body knows. If the breath is short and the mouth is dry, it means you haven't yet convinced your nervous system that the lion is gone. So we start there. Not with mantras, not with meaning. With moisture.

I've coached CEOs whose voices cracked before every presentation, not from nerves—but from a dry mouth silently screaming, 'We're under threat.' I've seen grieving parents whose eyes refused to water because their system was stuck in such deep freeze that even tears had nowhere to go. So we thaw.

First, through breath—low and slow, coaxed rather than commanded. Then, through sound. Humming, sighing, soft vowel sounds—all of them rippling through the vagus nerve like tuning forks through a frozen lake. Then comes the tongue.

The drop of the tongue—so minor it seems absurd—turns out to be the secret switch. Held high against the roof of the mouth, the tongue is a signal of readiness, of bracing. But when it drops, resting like a lazy passenger at the bottom of your mouth, it sends a message upstream: no more attack expected. We are not leaping, lunging, or explaining. We are landing.

Try it. Let the tongue fall. Then notice your jaw. Your breath. Your shoulders. The floor beneath your feet. Everything shifts half an inch toward ease. This isn't relaxation in the spa-day sense. It's physiological readiness—for life, not just survival. It's the difference between gripping and holding. Between collapsing and yielding.

The signal of fluids is a conversation with your body, in its native tongue. The more you notice it, the more fluent you become. Dryness means vigilance. Moisture means return.

This is why singers, wind players, and old-school orators often have better resilience than they realise. Not because they're brave, but because their artform *requires* the tongue and breath to drop and the mouth to wet. They train the very systems most people neglect.

And in doing so, they keep the signal alive. Because the goal isn't just to calm down. It's to come back online.

The signal of fluids is not symbolic. It's operational. It's your body's litmus test. And when you learn to read it—when you learn to *trust* it—you no longer need to guess whether you're coping. You'll know. Not in your thoughts, but in your tissues. In the taste at the back of your throat. In the shimmer behind your eyes. In the strange, miraculous fact that the body *always* knows before you do.

So listen. And when you hear the whisper of moisture returning, don't rush it. Don't reach for meaning. Just notice. *And begin again.*

FIVE

THE DELIGHT
JOY ISN'T A PLACE. IT'S A PRACTICE.

Delight is not the opposite of grief.
It is its companion, if allowed.

JOY CAN BEGIN AGAIN—HERE. Not in euphoria, but in mischief. Not in arriving at some distant place called "healed", but in the flicker of return: a laugh that escapes, a sway that surprises, a grin that breaks through.

In this chapter, we shift from safety to celebration—not the loud kind, but the kind that bubbles up sideways, like music through a wall. We've walked the long road of shutdown and re-entry. Now, we rehearse delight. Not as denial of grief, but as its counterbalance. Because to laugh while grieving is not betrayal. It's resistance. It's recovery. It's rhythm.

Music, Movement & Reconnection

It's hard to stay stuck when the hips start to move. Not impossible—some people can brace through a Beyoncé concert—but biologically speaking, rhythm is rebellion against freeze: mobilisation is an antidote to immobilisation.

Movement, breath, vibration: these are the original language of safety, long before we hired words to do the job. You don't soothe a child by explaining Keynesian economics. You hum. You rock. You sway. You sync. So does your nervous system.

There's a reason the old spirituals were sung in chains. A reason battle drums preceded the battle. A reason church choirs, jazz solos, marching bands, and raves all do the same thing: they don't just entertain. They regulate. They say,

> *'You are not alone. We're moving through this together.'*

It's also why grief makes statues of us. Frozen throat. Locked jaw. Rigid hips. The breath retreats, the body stiffens, and the music goes mute. The answer is not to think your way out of shutdown. It's to *sing* your way out. Or hum. Or blow into a flute like your life depends on it—because sometimes it does.

Singing isn't about talent. It's about tone. And tone is vibration. When you sing, you massage the throat from the inside. You coax the jaw into letting go. You soften the back of the mouth where the tongue clenches. In anatomical terms: you are hijacking your own stress reflex with resonance.

A client once told me he couldn't get past the loss of his wife. I didn't argue. I listened. I asked about her—her laugh, her scent, her music. 'Johnny Cash,' he said:

> *'She made me dance to Johnny Cash.'*

His eyes welled. His mouth tightened. I asked when he last danced. He laughed in that bitter, bone-dry way that says 'Never again.'

So, I told him the truth:

> *'You're not honouring her. You're dying beside her.'*

He blinked. I added,

> *'But maybe you don't need to "get over" her. Maybe you need to get under the music again. Maybe your body remembers the steps even if your mind's still in black and white.*
>
> *Because* 'you've got to move when you feel the blues''

Because movement *is* memory. The hips don't lie, as someone once said—though in my experience, they sulk, lock, and hold back like unpaid council workers when grief has lodged itself in the system. Unclenching the hips is not just physical. It's ancestral. It's where terror hides when it can't find the exit.

Wind players know this. So do singers. So do toddlers who rock themselves to sleep in orphanages. The out-breath, the drop of the diaphragm, the squeeze and release of the pelvic muscles—these aren't trivial acts. They're ancient declarations:

'We are not dead yet.'

Try humming with your lips closed and your hand on your chest. Feel the vibration. Try blowing through a straw as if summoning calm through a milkshake. Try dancing—not for the crowd, not for the calories—but for the circuitry. Try moving your jaw, stretching your tongue, bouncing your knees in a kitchen nobody else has to see.

This isn't art. It's reconnection. Because the body keeps the score—but rhythm writes the reply.

Finding Meaning Without Losing the Frame

Some beliefs arrive like handwritten notes; others like legal contracts. The trouble is, the brain rarely distinguishes between the two. It treats both as gospel—especially under duress. Especially in grief.

He said it plainly. Not with defiance or despair. Just... fact. As if gravity had issued a press release. We were sitting in a room that smelled faintly of tea and scorched sorrow.

He wasn't crying. That part had calcified. What he was doing was worse: narrating the loss on loop, like a bedtime story for someone who no longer slept.

'I'll never get over her.'

Now, you could take that sentence and rearrange it like bad IKEA furniture—probe the 'never', question the 'get over', yank at the implications like they were loose threads in a jumper. But that misses the point. The sentence wasn't just structure. It was scaffolding. Keeping the whole thing—grief, guilt, memory—upright.

So instead, I asked him to tell me about her. He did. Her laugh. The way she danced barefoot to Johnny Cash. The way she taught him how to cook—not by instruction, but by pouring wine and saying 'just feel it'.

He told me about their wedding, and how the DJ played 'Ring of Fire' at exactly the wrong moment. And he smiled. Not performatively. Reflexively. The way you smile when your body remembers joy before your brain gives permission.

I let the sentence sit for a while—'I'll never get over her'—and then I asked, gently:

> 'But what if you didn't have to get over her?'

He blinked.

> 'What if you honoured her by dancing again?'

He laughed once—sharp, like a door creaking open. 'To Johnny Cash?'

> 'As a starting point.'

Later, I said this:

> 'You've been treating sorrow as your duty. But
>   maybe love doesn't ask for that kind of
>   loyalty. Maybe she didn't want a statue.
>   Maybe she wanted music.'

He wept. And somewhere in that weeping, something cracked—usefully.

Because here's what grief warps: not just your heart, not just your timeline, but your map of meaning. The internal GPS that once said 'Turn left for joy' now loops endlessly through cul-de-sacs of 'Never again' and 'If only'. But maps, like beliefs, can be redrawn.

A month later, he called. He'd been dancing. Badly. Joyfully. We both cried (though only one of us admitted it).

The trick is to notice when the structure is choking the content. When 'I failed' starts swallowing everything else—every gesture, every memory, every breath that isn't an apology. I once worked with a man who said:

> *'I'm not the man I used to be.*
> *I've failed. I'm buckling. I'm lost.'*

He said it like a line from a Greek chorus. And who was I to argue? Except... his eyes told a different story. His spine, even in its slump, held something uncollapsed.

So I asked, not accusingly but curiously:

> *'When you crawled through the last hell, did you*
> *have a map then? Or did you grope your way*
> *out?'*

He stared. Said nothing. But his body replied—sat up straighter, drew breath like someone who'd just been handed a rope.

That's the game here—not to correct the grammar of grief, but to loosen it. To ask whether the frame is still useful, or whether it's become a cage.

Because our life's details are our story. Structure is the shape we force it into. And when grief strikes, both tend to warp.

The belief that 'It'll always be like this.'

The story that 'I'm to blame.'

The sentence that ends too early, or loops endlessly without punctuation.

We don't need to tear those apart. We need to listen to their rhythm. Feel their pressure. And then—sometimes with humour, sometimes with scalpel precision—we begin to reshape the frame. Not to distort the truth, but to make room for the rest of it.

Because grief, left unframed, can become the only content we see. But grief, gently framed, can make room for something else. Like dancing. Or laughter. Or remembering without breaking. Like life—not beyond grief, but beside it.

Notice. Shift. Surrender.

Relapse is a cruel word. Too clinical. Too final. It suggests failure—an undoing, a fall from grace. As if you'd scaled the mountain, planted your flag, and then, without warning, slipped all the way back to the bottom. But grief doesn't deal in linear progress. There's no summit. No straight trail. Just terrain—some of it familiar, most of it newly cruel—and the occasional illusion of altitude.

Better, then, to think in spirals. Because that's what it is, most days. A loop. A return with a difference. You come back to the ache, yes—but not as the same person. Not with the same breath. Not with the same grip on the handrail. You're looping—

but you're higher on the spiral. Sometimes only by a fraction. Sometimes by a hair's breadth. But higher all the same.

And if you can hold that—really hold it—you'll stop mistaking the spiral for a setback. You'll start seeing it as the system checking its notes. Running a systems test. Stress-testing the welds on your still-soft recovery.

But even spirals need maintenance. They don't climb themselves. Which is why this next part matters—not as a theory, but as a practice. A cycle. A script for the body. Three steps: *Notice. Shift. Surrender.*

That's the fluid spiral. The one that doesn't snap. The one that holds you when everything else is failing its audition.

Notice.

The signs never start where you expect. Not in the dramatic sob or the shouted memory. They start in the corners. The pauses. The micro-signals you've trained yourself not to see.

The jaw clenches. The tongue lifts to the roof of your mouth. Your vision narrows. Your breath shortens. Not a gasp. Not a heave. Just a barely-there tightening—as if your lungs are trying not to make a fuss.

You forget the last thing you tasted. You blink less. You stare longer. You speak a little too quickly, or not at all. And somewhere in the middle of all that, a small voice says: *Something's off.* But it gets drowned out. By routine. By urgency. By the thousand tasks of pretending to be okay.

So we slow it down. We start by listening for the first betrayal— the one your body makes against softness. The dryness of the mouth. The tension behind the eyes. The half-held breath that thinks it's being helpful. This is your cue. This is where the spiral can either descend or rise.

SHIFT.

You don't win a panic attack. You don't out-think your way out of freeze. What you do—what we teach the system to do—is shift. Not dramatically. Not heroically. Just... slightly. Enough to interrupt the automatic. Enough to say,

'Wait. Let me steer.'

The shift starts with the tongue. Drop it. Let it rest like a hammock at the bottom of your mouth. Let gravity have it. The moment you do, the jaw follows. Then the breath. Then the shoulders. It's a chain reaction, if you let it be.

Next, the pelvic floor. The part of you that most of you forget exists—until it braces like the bottom of a falling lift. Gently squeeze. Then release. Not as a workout. As a signal of calm and peace.

Then sigh. A long, low exhale. A King Henry VIII-style exorcism of tension. If the sigh sounds performative, it's working. Because part of you is still performing for the world, and another part is finally asking to be real.

And finally: breathe in *as if* you're slurping a noodle. Silly is helpful here. Because play is the opposite of panic. It's hard to spiral downward when you're trying not to laugh at yourself. The body doesn't do fear and fun at the same time. It has to choose.

So make it choose fun. Or at least farce. That's the shift.

Surrender.

This is the part we're worst at. We'd rather push, analyse, reframe, resist. Surrender sounds like losing. Like giving up. But in practice, surrender is where the repair happens.

Because once the body's signal begins to soften—once the breath is low, the jaw loose, the floor beneath you suddenly more solid—you don't need to *do* anything. You need to stop doing. Stop fixing. Stop bracing for the next emotional ambush. Let go of the handlebars. Trust the road. Trust the spiral.

Surrender doesn't mean collapse. It doesn't mean passive acceptance of suffering. It means relaxing your grip just enough to let the system do what it knows how to do: *recalibrate*. You've done the noticing. You've done the shifting. Now you let the current carry you.

It may only last a minute. A breath. A blink. But in that moment, you've risen. Not out of grief—but through it. And that's the whole point.

The spiral isn't a symbol. It's a tool. A way to name the messy return without losing your place. A way to climb even while doubling back. And each time you complete the loop—*notice, shift, surrender*—you stretch the distance between spirals. You bend the trajectory toward something that, eventually, looks like forward.

So when the next wave hits—and it will—don't ask why you're back here. Just ask:

Where am I now on the spiral?

Then begin again. Quietly. Deliberately. Like someone who knows the way.

Joy is **a Discipline**

Somewhere along the cultural assembly line, we swallowed a lie with our *Weet-Bix*: sorrow is noble; joy is frivolous. We learned to speak grief fluently and laugh in whispers—as though sadness were tax-deductible and delight a luxury for the underemployed. You can wear black and be taken seriously. Try dancing in a supermarket and see how quickly security takes an interest.

But here's the truth, though it arrives awkwardly and without proper credentials: joy is no less real than sorrow. No less earned. No less rehearsed.

We don't fall into joy like it's a romantic comedy trope. We learn it the same way we learn despair: by doing it often enough that our body begins to anticipate it. Grief becomes automatic because it's practised. *So, must joy.*

The idea that happiness should be spontaneous is not just wrong—it's strategically disabling. It sets people up to fail. Like telling someone to bench press a piano without ever showing them the gym. And when they strain or stumble or can't lift it, they assume they're defective. When, really, they just haven't trained.

You've heard of muscle memory. Joy has one too. But most of us keep trying to summon it like it's a genie—three wishes, no preparation, and please hurry up because the mortgage is late.

What if, instead, we treated joy like grief's cleverer sibling—less dramatic, more consistent? What if it wasn't the opposite of sorrow, but the counterbalance? Not a denial of what's gone wrong, but a rehearsal for what could still go right?

I remember the first laugh after Mark died. It wasn't generous. It was mean. Something sarcastic muttered under my breath at a police officer's expense. I smiled like I'd committed a crime. It felt alien. Disrespectful. But it wasn't. It was survival pushing through a hairline crack.

Years later, when Kieran died, I didn't laugh for weeks. My voice shrank to a whisper. Then one morning, Gillian tripped over the laundry basket and swore with such creative venom that I barked a laugh before I could stop myself. It wasn't a pretty laugh. It didn't heal me. But it reminded my lungs that their job wasn't just to inflate. They could lift.

That's where joy begins again—not in euphoria, but in mischief. Not in triumph, but in the small acts that say,

> *'I'm still here. And I can still feel something*
> *other than collapse.'*

So, I began rehearsing. Not in secret. Not in shame. In full view of the ordinary. Music in the kitchen. Podcasts in the car. Silliness scheduled with the same rigour I used to reserve for mourning. And it felt ridiculous at first. Like dragging your legs through treacle to do a cartwheel. But here's the thing:

> *Your body doesn't need a reason to move. It needs permission.*

Because the movement itself *is* the reason in and of itself.

I made playlists. Not curated for taste, but for effect. Brass bands. Funk. Scottish folk songs sung by drunk uncles. Anything with a rhythm strong enough to override the hesitation. I danced. Badly. Often. Once in a hardware store, just to prove to myself I wasn't dead.

I started humming in queues, sighing in public, and laughing at things that wouldn't pass a comedy test. I called it 'scheduled silliness'. Not because I was pretending all was well, but because I needed a reason not to dissolve.

One client of mine—recently widowed—told me she'd stopped smiling because it felt disloyal. As though *'joy' means 'forgetting'*. I told her this:

> *'If your husband had died saving a stranger,*
> *would you honour him by never smiling*
> *again?*
> *Or by being the sort of person whose joy reflects*
> *his courage?'*

She blinked. Paused. Then asked for permission to wear red again.

Grief is greedy. It'll take every corner of your life if you let it. But joy—joy's patient. It waits for an opening. And when you give it one—when you practice it like you once practiced sorrow

—it learns to show up on time. Not always. Not flawlessly. But enough to remind you: this, too, is part of you.

Delight is not a betrayal. It's a birthright. And like every skill, it strengthens under repetition. You get better at what you do often. So do what brings you life. Not because it fixes the damage. But because it keeps you human while you heal.

DELIGHT IS **a Practice**

You don't drift into joy. Not reliably. Not after loss.

Grief, as we've established, is a master of rehearsal. It doesn't show up out of nowhere—it's trained, disciplined, bloody punctual. Grief gets up early, stretches its metaphors, and practises in the mirror until it knows your angles.

That ache in your chest? *Rehearsed.* That hollowness in the morning? *Practised.* Your whole system, from breath to blink, has spent months (or years) perfecting the choreography of pain. Which is why delight needs its own warm-up routine.

We tend to talk about joy like it's a weather pattern. If you're lucky, it rolls in. If not, stay inside and look mournful. But joy—real joy—isn't meteorological. It's physiological. And it's trainable. Which means it's your job, whether you feel like it or not, to put it through its paces.

Think of it like this: you're not a failure for not feeling joy automatically. You're a *white-belt*. You've just begun. And your opponent—shutdown, despair, numbness—is a black-belt with tenure. It knows every trick. It's been doing press-ups while you were trying to breathe. So of course delight doesn't arrive unannounced. It's not rude. It's just under-practised.

That's where ritual comes in. Not candles and chants (unless that's your thing). I mean warm-ups. Micro-rituals. Little acts of deliberate kindness toward your nervous system. Not to impress anyone. Not to perform gratitude. But to rehearse a state your body has forgotten how to access on its own.

Start simple. Post-shower, before you re-enter the noise of the day, try this: drop your jaw. Let your tongue rest like a hammock. Breathe low. Now hum—lips closed, chest vibrating, like you're tuning your own circuitry. This isn't mystical. It's mechanical. You're telling your body: the war is over. We can proceed to living.

Then, add movement. Nothing dramatic. You're not auditioning for *So You Think You Can Grieve*. Just something to unstick the hips. A twist. A sway. A ridiculous stretch with an even more ridiculous noise. This is not about elegance. It's about signal. Movement says:

'I'm not frozen. I belong to life again.'

Now voice. Try it while brushing your teeth or waiting for the kettle. Speak something warm. Out loud. A line of poetry. A favourite lyric. A joke so bad it makes you snort. Let your throat remember it's allowed to vibrate for reasons other than defence or explanation.

Sing, if you can. If not, whisper with rhythm. The point is not volume—it's vibration. The point is tone. Your body listens to tone.

This is the rewiring. Not a lightning strike. A series of fuses, rewoven. Breath by breath. Day by day. Not because joy deserves your effort—but because *you do*.

And here's the sneaky bit. Once you've done this enough times, the body begins to cue you. Like a dog dragging you toward the park. The ritual becomes reflex. The hum before coffee. The breath before email. The sway before the school run. No one sees it, but you feel it—a brief flicker of 'I'm here. I'm still me.' *That's delight.* Not giddy or loud. Just present. Just warm.

Of course, you'll forget. You'll skip days. You'll get busy being responsible or broken or both. But the body forgives repetition far more than it rewards guilt. Just start again. Midday, midnight, Monday. Doesn't matter. Repetition is redemption. Joy doesn't need to be constant—it just needs to be familiar.

And if you're the sort who rolls your eyes at journaling (hello, fellow cynic), let me offer a reframe: don't record what you're grateful for. Record what felt good enough to repeat. One line. No adjectives. No insight. Just:

- 'The sunlight on the toaster.'
- 'The joke in the queue.'
- 'The breath that came back like it meant it.'

These are not moments of reflection. They're blueprints. Traces of your own return. Because here's what I believe:

> *After loss, after the pit, after the prison: joy is not a miracle. It's a muscle. And like any muscle, it gets stronger when worked.*

> *Not heroically. Not aesthetically. Just consis-*

*tently. With enough small reps to make it
reflex.*

You don't wait for delight. You train for it.

So pick your practice. Choose your cues. Hum, breathe, move, mutter. Be daft. Be private. Be unashamed. Because every time you do, you're not just fighting grief. You're teaching your body how to come back. And if that's not worthwhile work, I don't know what is.

The Quiet Miracle of Breathable Life

You don't come back the same. You don't walk out of the pit with your shirt tucked and your soul ironed flat, ready to slot back into the Before. There is no Before. Not anymore. That shape won't hold. The grief saw to that.

But neither do you emerge as rubble. You don't stay cracked. Or brittle. Or stuck in the chapel of past tense. What happens—if you're lucky, and stubborn, and surrounded just enough—is this: *you thaw*.

Not all at once. Not with cinematic grace. Not with strings swelling behind you like some third-act redemption arc. Just a breath. Then another. A slow return to the idea that the world might still want you in it—and that you, against all better judgement, might want to be here too.

Resilience, in this light, is not armour. It's not the brave face you strap on like a helmet. It's not coping via clenched jaw and inbox zero. It's not even strength in the way we usually mistake it—stoic, steel-spined, uninterested in softness.

Resilience is stretch. Elasticity. The capacity to deform and reform without breaking. Not because you were untouched, but because you were touched deeply—and moved anyway.

We get told that grief defines you. But that's not quite right. Grief *distorts* you. It warps the shape of how you speak, sit, hope. And resilience is what allows the warp to become part of your design—not a flaw, but a fold. A learned curvature that knows how to carry weight without buckling again.

You're not 'getting over it'. That's a phrase best left to flatpack furniture and bad dates. What you're doing is far more audacious. You are learning to breathe again. Not the kind of breath that gets you through a board meeting. The kind that arrives unannounced in the kitchen, in the bath, in the quiet aftermath of not crying. The kind of breath that no longer asks if it's allowed.

That is the miracle. Not fireworks. Not catharsis. Just the return of breath that doesn't need permission.

I've watched it happen in others. I've felt it happen in myself. The return is never grand. It sneaks in. Mid-step. Mid-sentence. Mid-sigh. And the only sign it's arrived is the almost-laugh—the startled exhale that says:

'I'm still here. Still breathing. Still, somehow, alive.'

That's the prize. Not closure. Not transcendence. Continuity. A breath that doesn't hurt.

You don't need to chase joy like a debt collector. You don't need to rush your recovery like it's an airport transfer. You just need to build space for the breath to arrive. To rehearse delight as often as you once rehearsed disaster. To let yourself be reshaped —not back into what was, but forward into what's next.

This whole journey—this *Back Into Delight*—isn't about solving grief. It's about staying soft enough to feel it, and elastic enough to keep moving. It's about becoming a body that knows how to re-enter connection, despite the wreckage. It's about remembering that grief may leave marks, but joy leaves muscle memory too.

And that memory—of safety, of laughter, of stillness—is your rope out of the pit. It is your blueprint for return. Because you don't transcend grief. You thaw around it. And each breath that arrives without effort? That's not nothing. That's a quiet miracle.

The Art of Staying

Delight doesn't always dance. Sometimes it sketches. Sometimes it scribbles in notebooks no one else reads. Sometimes it builds, sings, or stitches together images from a life before rupture.

When movement feels like too much and silence starts to splinter, creative expression offers another way through. It doesn't demand performance. It doesn't expect clarity. It simply invites contact—between breath and meaning, between memory and imagination, between body and world. This is not art therapy. It's *neurobiology* in motion.

Self-expression works because it speaks every dialect of the system:

- Our *reptile brain* calms when rhythm is steady—when the body rocks, or repeats, or presses colour onto paper.
- Our *mammal brain* is soothed by connection—by story, symbol, metaphor, memory.
- Our *primate brain* lights up in both hemispheres—naming, shaping, feeling, organising, dreaming.

When you paint, write, strum, rhyme, drum, or speak from the ache—you're not escaping it. You're staying with it. You're giving form to what has none. And in doing so, you create signal. Signal of life, signal of agency, signal of return.

That's why poems matter. Not because they rhyme. But because they pulse.

That's why stories help. Not because they resolve. But because they hold.

And that's why even a strange, half-hummed tune in the kitchen at 2 a.m. might be the most important thing you do all week.

It's not about being good. It's about being here. And when the page listens, or the guitar responds, or the brush finally lands just right—it's not just art. It's proof: *you stayed.*

S<small>AFE</small>, and Gently Resetting

To further reinforce this process, consider engaging in regular relaxation and centring practices. They don't need to take much time and, which can help dissolve any lingering discomfort.

I was asked to give a colleague a 'trance under 10' in a hotel lobby in Orlando, Florida. This is a recording, *Neuro-Spa*, is of that moment: just cleaned up and visually enhanced.

Scan this QR Code to listen it it, as it brings together lots of the elements we've discussed in less that ten minutes. It's a gentle and easy way to move from the 'idea' of altering your state to just doing it.

Neuro-Spa

It can be done 'eyes open' or 'eyes closed'. Because it is so fast, take the time and try it both ways. Coming in and out of an altered state, trains your neurology to do it deliberately. Practice, in other words

Through repetition, you're not just increasing your skill—you're training your mind to think in a new way, your body to feel a new way, which will lead you to begin to do new things; like moving *back into delight*, again and again. Because delight is a practice not a place.

THIS TOO IS RECOVERING

On the next page, you'll find a poem I wrote in the days after Kieran died. It wasn't planned. It wasn't structured. It simply came. And in that moment, it was the most raw and personal thing I had ever written.

At the time, I sensed it would help me heal. In hindsight, it was the catalyst—the first unbuckling of my inner *Stretch Armstrong*. Not because it removed the pain, but because it gave the pain somewhere to go. Onto a page. Outside my body.

This poem isn't an answer. It's just a handrail—held out by artful self-expression. And whatever form that takes for you, it matters. Self-expression helps us gain perspective—on where we are, who we are, what matters most now, and where we might go next.

Recovery is not a straight line. We spiral and bend our way through grief in our own time, in our own way. The invitation is simple: *notice, shift, and surrender*.

If you're walking with grief, I hope this poem offers a small prompt—a way to notice where you are on the spiral and orient yourself gently there. To express something. And in that act, to shift. To soften. To begin to return.

I reprint this for my boy, Kieran—and for those who stay.

With a Coffee in My Hand

Running over sand, splashing in water, there were wonderful times with my son and daughter.

They'd laugh out loud and I'd say "I'm proud"; and I'd say "yes" to everything they weren't allowed.

Chatting over pizza, giggling by the 'roos, cautious for a huntsman lurking in the loos.

Bags of sweets and gold class seats. Flickering wonders and some after-show treats.

Climbing on the Bridge, we're on top of the world! A man, a woman, a boy and a girl.

We'd plunge in the pool, go from hot to cool; under blue skies, we were playing the fool.

Driving to their house in an old grey van, I went to pick up my girl to help her career plan.

I didn't know that they had prepared to go. With the door ajar, I walked in slow.

My mouth was dry and my hands were cold; and I rescued some colours that were already rolled.

Noxious with fears, blinded by tears, unsteady on my feet and feeling my years.

Sitting on the step, abandoned and alone, I got into the van and made my way home.

The world bled away into a monochrome of grey; my cherubs had flown away that day.

. . .

BUT I STILL DREAMT OF them with their biggest grins, I would grab them and squeeze them and pull them in.

They'd laugh out loud and I'd say "I'm proud"; and I'd say that I've seen their faces in every crowd.

The barbie would smoke and the chops would spit, I'd cook them a feast and they'd scoff all of it.

They'd splash about. They'd scream and shout. They'd shower and wash and then laze about.

With the dawning sun, the revery would go; and they reverted to people that I used to know.

My heart would break, repair and ache. With a coffee in my hand, I had a dollar to make.

SHE WALKED through the room with pain on her face. I was told of his death, the time and the place.

My addled brain heard "ship" and "train". I discovered that I would never see my son again.

My breathless chest resisted air and I wished that an atheist could believe in prayer.

But the thought was token, no prayers were spoken. My boy's strong body was frozen and broken.

I lay dazed, numb and feeling sick because of the truth revealed on that gamer's joystick.

I dropped on a chair. I could only stare; and I conjured my father and our sons right there.

. . .

AND IF HE was standing there with his biggest grin, I would grab him and squeeze him and pull him in.

He'd laugh out loud and I'd say "I'm proud"; and I'd say that I've seen his face in every crowd.

But against blunt reality all fantasies lose; and mine were lost once I could process the news.

It was mental torture each time I sought a connection with my gentle son and beautiful daughter.

Perhaps the pain will never subside until I have endlessly cried and my tears have dried.

Empty in side. Stripped of all pride. Only with the last breath, when I have sighed and died.

UNTIL THAT DAY FROM NOW, I will carry my pain; my life, unchanged, will not be the same.

I'm a long way from Fife but I have a wonderful life, a daughter from Oz and a beautiful wife.

We have years of wonder, under blue skies above, and, wherever we wander, we will live with love.

They'll laugh out loud and I'll say "I'm proud"; and we'll live lives of joy as our wedding vowed.

A new day will come with the dawning sun and I shall recall my elder daughter and my only son.

My heart will break, repair and ache. With a coffee in my hand, I'll have a dollar to make.

AFTERWORD

I didn't write this book because I triumphed over grief. I wrote it because I fell into the pit twice and somehow came back carrying notes. Not conclusions. Not certainties. Just a rope tethered to something solid—and the decision not to keep it to myself.

This wasn't a grand act of generosity. It was survival, shared. I've sat across from too many parents with the same glazed stare, the same vanished breath, the same unasked question in their posture:

Am I still allowed to live?

You can't un-hear that question once you've recognised it. You can't nod politely and move on. You either stay with them in the pit, or you find a way to pass the ladder. That's what this book is: not an answer, but a ladder passed quietly between hands that know what it means to fall.

But let's be clear about something: we've been sold a terrible map. You've probably heard of the five stages of grief. Denial. Anger. Bargaining. Depression. Acceptance.

Clean. Sequential. Tidy. Comforting, in the way a laminated flowchart might be when your house is on fire. Except it wasn't written for mourners. It was written for the dying.

Elisabeth Kübler-Ross developed the model by interviewing terminally ill patients who were facing their own death—not people who had lost someone. The stages were never meant to explain how the living carry on.

And yet, the model got picked up, spread around, repackaged for mass consumption, and quietly mistaken for gospel. It shows up in training manuals, therapy brochures, TV scripts. We nod along, hoping our pain might at least follow instructions.

But grief doesn't. It stutters. It loops. It holds still for years, then trips you in the cereal aisle because someone coughs like your father used to.

There are no stages. There are reflexes. There are signals. There is shutdown. There is the return of breath. And there is the quiet miracle of remembering how to laugh without guilt.

The trouble with tidy models is they imply we should be tidier than we are. And that makes people think they're failing at grief —because they're not progressing. But grief doesn't resolve. It recalibrates. It bends our world, then invites us to move differently through it.

This isn't a linear journey. It's a physiological one. That's why the tools in this book start with breath, with sound, with muscle. You can't affirm your way out of numbness. You can't think your way back into joy. The nervous system isn't a whiteboard. It's a cave. You call out, you listen for the echo, and eventually, if you're lucky and a little absurd, the echo changes shape.

What I've offered here is not a manual—it's a kind of field guide for warped travellers. I can't tell you how long the journey will take, or how many times you'll freeze again. But I can tell you this:

Recovery isn't about transcendence. It's about *return*.

Not to who you were, but to motion. To elasticity. To range. You don't need to become someone new to heal. You need to *stretch back into yourself*.

And that's the strange privilege of walking with grief a second time. You learn that it doesn't obey any structure but its own— but you also learn how to interrupt its gravity.

I've seen it happen. I've seen the breath return. I've seen the jaw unclench. I've seen humour—wild, irreverent, uninvited—break through someone's face like sunlight through boarded windows. Those aren't moments of progress. They're moments of *reconnection*.

So if you've made it this far—if you've read through memories, metaphors, science, and sighs—I want to thank you. Not for finishing the book, but for staying with your body long enough to notice where it softened.

I hope something in these pages landed somewhere beneath your ribs and quietly changed the temperature. This isn't the end of grief. But it might be the end of isolation. It might be the moment you stop searching for the "right stage" and start noticing the *right signals*.

It might be the permission you didn't know you were waiting for: to laugh, to stretch, to move, to breathe—without needing a reason more noble than life itself. So no, I won't tell you to find closure. That word's done enough damage. But I will tell you this:

> *You are not broken. You been bent. And bent*
> *things don't need fixing.*

They need warmth. They need space. They need time. And sometimes, they need someone to say—preferably with a sigh and a sideways smile—

"My friend, you're not a spoon. You're a *Stretch Armstrong*."

Thank you for reading.

Turn the page when you're ready.

I'll be waiting just beyond it.

NOTE FROM THE ROAD

If you've made it this far, you've already done more than most.

Not because you finished the book—but because you stayed. With the ache. With the silence. With yourself. That's not nothing. That's practice. And practice is what recovery is built from —not progress charts or perfect days, but the quiet decision to begin again.

You may not feel different yet. That's alright. You may still ache, still clench, still pause before speaking their name aloud. That's also alright. The tools are not demands. They're invitations. Signals to the system that it's safe enough to soften. Safe enough to laugh. Safe enough to return.

Not to how things were. That world is gone. But to yourself. To life. To something stretchable, breathable, and new—not in content, perhaps, but in shape.

Grief doesn't disappear. It integrates. It settles into the rhythm. Not as weight, but as tempo. And you—strange, soft, elastic creature that you are—are learning to move with it.

So here's what I'll say from this part of the path:

> *If today you manage a sigh, if tomorrow you*
> *manage a stretch, and if one day,*
> *unprompted, joy wanders in through the*
> *back door—just let it come in.*

> *You don't have to explain.*

Just breathe. Just hum. Just sway. You are not broken.

_____

> *You're just finding home again.*

_____

Paul O'Neill.

November 2022

IN MEMORY OF

My son, Kieran O'Neill

My brother, Mark O'Neill

My father, Hugh O'Neill

My aunt, Helen Miles

My aunt, Anita Monro

My uncle, Adam O'Neill

My mentor, Tim Dalmau

My friend, Caroline Kelly

My friend, Jack Keogh

Loved. Missed. Remembered.

NOTES & RESOURCES

This book was written from life. But some of the tools it draws on have lineage—neuroscience, therapeutic models, and somatic practices that gave structure to what might otherwise have stayed as instinct.

The sources below are not academic endorsements. They're scaffolding. If you're curious to explore more deeply—or share this work with others—these references will give you the maps behind the metaphors.

The Neuro-Linguistic Programming Roots

Frogs Into Princes (Bandler & Grinder, 1979)

Trance-Formations (Bandler & Grinder, 1981)

These early works form the foundations of NLP—a field born from observing and modelling highly effective therapists. NLP tools have shown remarkable value in grief, state change, and rapid pattern disruption.

Chapters 3 and 4 borrow heavily from this lineage, especially around submodalities (the internal "code" of experience), anchoring, and the use of language to shift state.

Get the Life You Want (Richard Bandler, 2008)

This book refines earlier NLP into something warmer, more accessible, and deeply personal. Here, Bandler makes the case that emotional change doesn't have to be slow or painful—it can be fast, structured, and even joyful. He goes deeper into *Neuro-Hypnotic Repatterning* (NHR)—his re-engineering of trance and memory work.

Many of the techniques in Chapter 3 (spin reversal, state stacking, emotional editing) reflect this evolution. The idea is simple, if a little rebellious: emotions are rehearsed patterns—and patterns can be rehearsed differently.

Much of the approach in *Back Into Delight*—especially the blend of humour and physiology—owes a clear debt to this work. If you're looking for a guide that feels both rigorous and human, start here.

The Elusive Obvious (Michael Grinder, 2003)

Michael Grinder taught me how to see breath, tone, and presence as visible signals—not abstract ideas. His notion of "permission-based communication" helped me build rapport with people who didn't yet trust words. He also taught me this: if someone isn't breathing low, they're not listening deeply. So change the breath, then speak.

The Brain's Plasticity & the Body's Promise

The Polyvagal Theory (Stephen Porges, 2011; *and distilled in 2017's Pocket Guide*)

Porges' research reshaped how we understand trauma, safety, and connection. His key insight? The nervous system is constantly scanning for cues—not through logic, but through breath, tone, and micro-expression. When the ventral vagal system is active, we feel safe enough to reach.

Much of Chapter 2 and Chapter 4 builds on this: breath, prosody, posture, and the unspoken question the body asks a hundred times a day—*"Am I safe enough to connect?"*

Bliss Brain (Dawson Church, 2020)

This work expands the conversation around neuroplasticity. Techniques like meditation, breathwork, and EMDR (Eye Movement Desensitisation and Reprocessing) don't just make us feel better—they rewire the brain. Boosting theta waves (a state linked to calm, learning, and integration) is part of what makes the trance work in *Chapter 3* effective—not mystical, just measurable.

The Body Keeps the Score (Bessel van der Kolk, 2014)

Though not directly quoted, van der Kolk's insight threads through this book: trauma is held in the body, not just the mind. His work overlaps with Polyvagal Theory and helps explain why grief is not just emotional, but physiological. Immobilisation is a survival strategy. Recovery requires movement—sometimes breath by breath.

The Elastic Return: Breath, Fluid & Body

Grief as Warping

The concept of "grief as warping" is developed here as a metaphor for nonlinear trauma response.

Readers may also find resonance in works on narrative identity and meaning-making after loss (e.g., Joan Didion, Megan Devine, David Kessler).

Mechanical Properties

Concepts like ductility, malleability, elasticity, and toughness are drawn from materials science and engineering.

They were used here as metaphors for emotional and physiological resilience.

Stretch Armstrong vs. Uri Geller – Cultural References

- Stretch Armstrong was a popular 1970s toy known for its extreme elasticity.
- Uri Geller gained fame (and controversy) for his televised spoon-bending demonstrations in the same era.

Speech & Singing as Autonomic Training – Humming, voice, fluidity

Professions like singing, acting, and wind playing naturally train regulation by engaging breath, low and forward tongue positioning, *back-of-the-throat* relaxation reflex, vagal tone, and oral signalling—core components of safe nervous system functioning.

<u>Putting it All Together</u>

The techniques shared—sighing like Henry VIII, breathing like a noodle slurper, spinning panic backwards with clown music—might seem absurd. That's on purpose. Absurdity loosens the grip of pattern. But they're also rigorously designed. Every laugh, every sound, every breath was tested—not just in workshops or coaching rooms, but in the middle of real heartbreak.

This book does not pretend to be definitive. It doesn't hand out closure or promise healing on a schedule. But it is precise in one belief: that recovery is possible when the body is invited back to the surface—safely, gently, and with a little mischief.

If you'd like to go further, the sources above are a good beginning. And if all you remember is this—that breath can lead the way, and laughter is allowed—then you've already come far.

ACKNOWLEDGMENTS

My thanks to the minds whose work has shaped this one.

To **Richard Bandler**, whose human-change technologies, tools and techniques have rewired not just others, but it brought me 'back into D'Light'. For that, I am forever grateful.

To **Michael Grinder**, for teaching me how to listen with my eyes. You give myself permission to heal myself at Tim's place and it made all the difference in the world.

To **Stephen Porges**, whose *Polyvagal* insights whisper beneath every breath in this book—even when unnamed. Your beautiful *science of safety* has change my life.

To **Dawson Church,** whose radiant research in *Bliss Brain* illuminated the neural pathways back to joy. For proving that even grief-scarred brains can rewrite their endings, thank you.

ABOUT THE AUTHOR

Paul O'Neill knows what it is to be buckled—and to begin again.

For over twenty-five years, he has guided individuals, teams, and organisations through complexity, crisis, and change. His work spans continents and sectors—corporate boardrooms, frontline hospitals, elite sports environments, mining sites, and classrooms—and his approach is grounded in one enduring truth: real change begins in the nervous system, not the strategy document.

Paul is a leadership consultant, neuro-resilience trainer, and coach trusted by professionals navigating pressure, grief, and uncertainty. Trained in the sciences of language, breath, and behaviour, he's known for helping people shift—gently but decisively—out of shutdown and into motion.

Back Into Delight is his most personal work. It wasn't written from theory, but from loss. Not from what he teaches, but from what he lived. This book is both a memoir and a map—for anyone learning how to breathe again after heartbreak.

He lives in Australia with his wife, Gillian, and daughter, Carmen, whose love remains the soft place he always returns to.

ALSO BY PAUL O'NEILL

.

Printed in Dunstable, United Kingdom